The Parable

of the

Shoes

(The Hidden Value of a Comfortable *Soul*)

Judy Reamer

with
Donna Alberta

Illustrated by
Bobbie Wilkinson

The Parable of the Shoes
(The Hidden Value of a Comfortable *Soul*)

Judy Reamer
with
Donna Alberta

Illustrated by
Bobbie Wilkinson

Copyright © 2003 by Judy Reamer
Printed in the United States of America
ISBN: ISBN 0-9744231-0-6
Editorial Assistance
By Donna Cornelius, WriteWorks Inc.

Table of Contents

The Parable of the Shoes

Dedication

To Pat Boone, the first comfortable shoe I ever knew, and the man who was destined by God to direct *my feet* onto paths of righteousness. For years, this worldwide entertainer has been wearing his signature white bucks, and one day they led him to walk alongside me as my spiritual father in the faith.

The Parable of the Shoes

Foreword

I had listened to Judy Reamer's riveting testimony on tape in the winter of 1996. It detailed the remarkably uncommon, and sometimes comical, account of her journey from Judaism to Christianity. (Do you know *anyone else* who was baptized by a celebrity in Las Vegas waters?) I also had read her insightful, one-of-a-kind book on lust, *Feelings Women Rarely Share.* I passed the book and a cassette of Judy's incredible salvation story on to a few other women's ministry leaders so they could hear it. In April, when planning our church's women's retreat, which would take place the following winter, we sensed that God had already provided the speaker.

Grand Rapids, Michigan was the site for our retreat. It was bitter cold that February when Judy arrived at the conference hotel. But we warmed up to her immediately! Her personality generated a kind of "holy heat rush" in the room (having absolutely *nothing* to do with the biochemical changes taking place in many of the women present.) Judy's creativity and wry sense of humor were immediately obvious. But we also quickly discovered she has a true genius for presenting easy-to-get-a-handle-on illustrations for hard-to-grasp theological concepts.

I loved her right from the start—first on tape, then in person. She's fun . . . and serious. She's brilliant . . . and humble. She's a teacher . . . and a learner. She's confident . . . and uncertain. She's strong . . . and weak. Judy Reamer is the kind of person I enjoy. She's easy to be with, open and honest, always ready to share a good laugh—or a good cry—with her friends. But the *best* thing about Judy is her obvious love for the Lord, and her desire to always make " . . . the teaching about God our Savior attractive" through her sensitive and winsome ways.

That's why I knew the vital lessons in Judy's seminar, *The Parable of the Shoes,* needed to become a book. The concepts she shares are critical to the mission of the church of Jesus Christ. In Matthew 28:19 God invites, or more accurately, *commands* us to join Him in reaching others with His love and teachings. How can we do this if we are offensive to others? . . . Insensitive or opinionated? . . . Consumed with self-interest? . . . Boorish or bothersome? . . . Controlling or contrary?

The Parable of the Shoes is a whimsical yet penetrating look at our personal responsibility to enhance, rather than hurt, the credibility of the Gospel. A good camaraderie often provides the best context for sharing the message of God's great gift of salvation. So what are you like? Are you like Judy? Are you easy to be with, comfortable to be around?

May this book help you understand not only the importance of the message, but of the messenger whose feet bring it. Bless your soul!

> *Stand firm then, with . . . your feet fitted with the readiness*
> *that comes from the gospel of peace.*
> *Ephesians 6:14–15*

Donna Rae Alberta
Brighton, Michigan

Parade of Shoes

On the street today I watched feet.
I saw the battered boots on a laborer.
A teen in baggy pants was shod in worn sneakers.
A young lady wore delicately strapped sandals.
An athletic young man wore a pair of athletic shoes
that must have set him back a hundred dollars.

I asked myself,
"Would I be willing to step into those shoes
and experiences they represent?
Could I know what it feels like
to be pushed by a boss to complete an impossible job?
How can I understand the world of today's teen?"

Successful human relationships depend on our willingness
to try to walk in another's shoes.
Jesus did.

The Scripture says He "made himself nothing,
taking the very nature of a servant,
being made in human likeness." (Philippians 2:7, NIV)

The Son of God willingly set aside His divinity,
left His Father's presence, and was born into a peasant family.
Being fully human, He understands us.

Now, He prays for us as a great High Priest
who is able to identify with our cries, our longings, our joys.
And as we walk through life,
we must show others that we care enough
to try on their shoes and walk with them.

By Pastor Jerry Scott
Washington Assembly of God, Washington, NJ

Introduction

"If we trusted God's wisdom, we would present our message in a manner that utilized every positive communication skill possible."
—Dr. James B. Richards[1]

Do you have good friends? I'd bet my Birkenstocks you would describe them as "The people I feel at ease with—no pretending, no awkwardness. I can share everything with them."

I'd say much the same about my friends. In fact, you're about to meet a whole bunch of my good friends. And although this book will be an easy read, a fun read, and I have smiled and chuckled my way along as I've written, please don't be fooled! My heart—and the book's content—have a deeply serious purpose in mind.

My goal is not to entertain you, but to challenge you in an entertaining way. To cause you to think about the critical nature of the mission God has entrusted to you and me—to be His messengers. And to realize the messenger is every bit as important as the message! He will see we have the right message, but God also wants to get His *messengers* right.

Rather than this book being a behavior-changing, self-help manual, may the Lord use this book to work a change in *us* where we need it. May He employ it so those who do not know Jesus will want to be in our company, enjoying Christ's fragrance which we wear, and because they would love to be in our shoes!

---

[1] Dr. James B. Richards, "How to Stop the Pain," Whitaker House

I believe with all my heart: **the extent to which others want to be around me usually is the extent to which God exacts His plan of mercy and love *through me* to anyone who crosses my path.** A corollary truth is that my attitudes and actions as a Christian can either make God look good, or damage the credibility of the Gospel for others.

This was on the heart of the Apostle Paul when he counseled Titus:

> *. . . teach the older women to be reverent in the way they live . . .*
> *to be kind, and to be subject to their husbands **so that no one will malign***
> ***the word of God.***
> *Titus 2:3, 5 (emphasis mine)*

> *Teach slaves to be subject to their masters in everything, to try to please*
> *them, not to talk back to them, and not to steal from them, but to show that*
> *they can be fully trusted, so **that in every way they will make the***
> ***teaching about God our Savior attractive.***
> *Titus 2:9–10 (emphasis mine)*

With the same objective in mind, Peter teaches that wives should be submissive to their husbands:

> *. . . so that, if any of them do not believe the word, **they may be won over***
> ***without words by the behavior of their wives. . . .***
> *1 Peter 3:1 (emphasis mine)*

Paul underscores the utility of being a comfortable person (an "old shoe" if you will) when he says:

. . . I make myself a slave to everyone, to win as many as possible. To the Jews I became like a Jew, to win the Jews . . . To those not having the law I became like one not having the law . . . so as to win those not having the law . . . I have become all things to all men so that by all possible means I might save some. I do all this for the sake of the gospel that I might share in its blessings.
1 Corinthians 9:19–23

Our Father doesn't live for our benefit. We are to live for His! Life is all about Him, always was, always is, and ever will be. John, "the apostle whom Jesus loved," said it best:

*"Thou art worthy, O Lord, to receive glory and honour and power: for thou hast created all things, and **for thy pleasure** they are and were created."*
Revelation 4:11 KJV (emphasis mine)

And now—

Welcome to Boot Camp!

SECTION ONE

When I Get Tired of Shopping, I Sit Down and Try on Shoes

The Parable of the Shoes

In a certain city, there was a high-class department store, L'Uppity's, known for its incredibly vast shoe department. Eager shoppers came great distances to experience its magic. To sell shoes, the owners went to great lengths to surround the shoppers with an alluring atmosphere of sensory delights: potpourri wafting, piano strains lilting, elegant sofas beckoning, gourmet coffees entreating, and fashionable personnel seducing.

The seekers were drunk with the power of the outward mystique. They staggered giddily from display to display. "Oooo! Ahhhh! I must see those shoes in my size." The shoes were ceremoniously delivered for inspection with personnel kneeling at the offered foot to slip on the shoe. The romance was beginning.

On the outskirts of that same city, stood a humble wooden store with a sign that simply read: "Sadie's Shoes." A "mom and pop" business with no apparent marketing savvy, its strategy was deep discounting. Its interior was as basic as its selling philosophy: towering racks overflowing, talk radio intruding, vinyl benches unwavering, vending machine humming, and cashier waiting.

The shoppers' adrenalin began pumping as Sadie barked over the loudspeaker, "Having a big sale today. Buy one, get one free."

"Yeah? Wow!" Hemmed in by narrow aisles, seekers were beginning to pull down boxes. The romance at this store also was beginning.

Throughout the day, smiling people emerged from each store with shoeboxes in tow. Satisfied expressions told the story of a happy ending for many shoppers. Their sole searching was over.

From Insole to Insight

When I get of tired of shopping, I "sits me down" and try on shoes, or . . . watch others try on shoes. At a mall with friends, I always suggest (if we separate to shop) that we regroup in the shoe section of a department store. That way, if I shop till I drop, I can plop, maybe try some shoes on, and have a place to sit and wait . . . and wait . . . and maybe even wait.

To me the shoe department is an interesting place to people-watch. The shoppers come in all shapes, colors, and sizes. Some fancy, some plain. Some give the impression of being worth more than others. *Some L'Uppity's; some Sadie's.*

One day, after carefully observing the selection of people on parade, I decided to look over the shoes on display. It suddenly occurred to me "the shoes were just like the people." Same description: all shapes, colors, and sizes. Some fancy, some plain. Some seemingly worth more than others.

I watched as people tried on, rejected, and sent back shoes. But eventually many shoppers sauntered over to the cashier to pay and walked out with a pair of shoes that pleased them. I saw the satisfied expressions on their faces and heard them genuinely thank the salesclerk. What had determined why each of these varied people had chosen a particular shoe? "What's *afoot* here?" I wondered.

"Aha!" I thought! It came to me when I began to put myself in their shoes. What drove *my* shoe selection? Was there a *sole* factor at work here?

The Soul Factor

The very first time I taught *The Parable of the Shoes,* I had an emergency strategy in mind. After spending more than twenty hours preparing the message, I realized its effectiveness hinged on *one* solitary word. If the attendees gave me the needed reaction, *collectively coming to a particular conclusion,* all my preparation would have been worth it. If my carefully formed agenda fell through, my emergency tactic would go into effect immediately. The "back-up plan" called for me to do just that—***back up*** to the nearest exit, weakly waving a "Buh-bye." Then I'd walk away from the ministry forever!

Before the retreat, a brochure had been mailed, clearly requesting all the women to wear their favorite shoes to the first session. The herd faithfully stomped into the auditorium sporting all kinds of footwear. Women who normally dressed carefully from head to toe had obviously dressed carefully only from head to ankle. But the shoes!!!!!! What a sight! The chosen shoes made no fashion sense when eyed with the outfit. If they had, some women would have had to don pajamas or a bathing suit. (Flip-flops were well represented.)

Dividing into small groups, the women were each to use a one-word description to justify her shoe choice. After fifteen minutes of discussion and straightening the chairs back into rows, all the ladies now eagerly lifted their gaze to *Mount Judy*. In their eyes, I could read, "*What was that exercise all about?*"

At the count of three, I asked them to yell out the word most commonly voiced during their "*shoe-bee, doo-bee*" conversations. My mouth was dry. My reputation was on the line. I bargained with God, "If you'll have these women, at this very moment, yell out the word on which my whole sermon hinges, I will become a missionary in Antarctica."

"One . . . two . . . three!" In unison, with no collaboration beforehand, they screamed, "COMFORTABLE!" I yelled back to them, "Yes!!!!! YESSS!!!!!" That was the word in my notes. It was the one word I had hoped they would say. Thank you, Lord! *Comfortable.* Just hearing them say the word made me feel at ease. I now moved closer to the microphone with renewed confidence, rather than retreating toward the exit.

Because of the experiment with those precious retreat "guinea pigs," I am able, with certainty, to present the key truth of *The Parable of the Shoes:* People choose shoes for comfort AND people choose "people" for comfort.

Each buyer had left L'Uppity's and Sadie's Shoes satisfied. Each had found shoes, which were "right" for her; which felt good. The shoes were also likely pleasing in color, style, and function. But *first,* the shoes felt great!

The shoes weren't purchased because of the fancy accoutrements of L'Uppity's or the deep discounting of Sadie's store. It was all about one word . . . **comfort!** Elegant shoes that were "to die for" were passed over at the fancy establishment. (Did you ever make such a fatal purchase, then wear them and say, "These shoes are *killing* me!"?) Shoes that were almost being given away at the "deal of a century" store were left sitting in the closet. (Been there, bought those, too! They're still in the box, cursed forever as "Those stupid cheap shoes that always rub me the wrong way.") The women wanted comfort first, a conforming to the foot, a sensitivity to the needs of their particular feet. They wanted a comfortable sole.

Much in the same way people look for comfortable *soles*, they are also on the lookout for comfortable *souls*. For a serious trek, people will reach in their closet for their most comfortable shoes; similarly they will reach out for the most comfortable people to walk them through life's weighty journeys to help them reach an eternal footing.

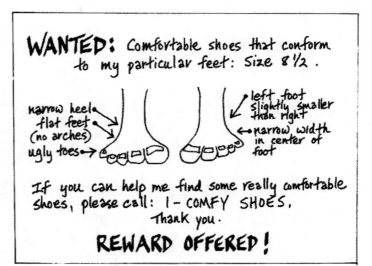

SECTION TWO

High Steppin' with the Lord

After me will come one more powerful than I, the thongs of whose sandals I
am not worthy to stoop down and untie.
John the Baptist, Mark 1:7

When it comes to comfort, let's first look at Jesus, the one Soul who marvelously fit himself to us when we were barefoot and naked in sin. As with your most comfortable shoe, He is the perfect resting place for your soul . . .

The Perfect Shoe

In the section to follow I will introduce you to some of my most comfortable shoes and some of my most comfortable friends. But before the parade of shoes begins, I would like to share with you my **most** comfortable shoe and friend.

My oldest pair of shoes will always have the same reputation . . . as my oldest pair of shoes. They will always be there for me. I shall not ever, *ever* part with my Space shoes. They have the distinct reputation of fitting only one person—me. And they fit me *perfectly.*

I had just given birth to our twins, Jill and Jeff, who were joining two other preschool age sons at home, Mark and Johnny. My legs and feet were hurting from the constant running or standing they had to endure in this hectic time of my life.

Sensibly, I succumbed to a cousin's insistence that I enter this tiny, unattractive store in downtown Baltimore to experience the saving grace of the Space shoe. I knew the seller was going to make a mold of my feet, so I shifted my body readying for the plaster impression.

"Sit down," the bespectacled, bald man commanded, "I need to get a mold of your feet."

"Why should I *sit* when I need support from the shoes when I am *standing?*"

"Because I want the mold to replicate your feet and legs while they are in a resting position."

In my most "Ah-ha!" tone, I agreed, saying, "Brilliant!!"

A couple of weeks later a package arrived at my home. Opening it, I spied the ugliest shoes I had ever seen. With unfashionable black leather exteriors, they were heavy, shaped oddly, and tied with laces. At first glance they didn't appear custom made. But, when I slipped my hand into one of the shoes, I knew. I could feel all the indentations of the toes, the ball of the foot, and the heel. When I slid my foot inside, what a wonderful surprise! The shoe satisfied my exact needs and brought rest to my sole.

I have worn and worn and worn those shoes . . . yet they haven't worn out. They hold my feet in place when I'm up and running, and yet they keep my feet in their position of rest. The shoes hug me securely, offering critical support where it's needed. Yet, they are roomy and spacey. They feel good, feel right, and feel safe. So much so, I had a pair made in white for the spring and summer seasons, too. Looking at their outward appearance, no one would be attracted to my Space shoes. If anyone else tried them on, the fit would be all wrong, because they were expressly made for one person named Judy Reamer.

When I wear these shoes I am reminded of Jesus Christ. He is *more* than all the close friends I have, rolled into one. God made Him to meet my exact needs and bring rest to my soul. As I have learned, there is no friend quite like Jesus. My relationship with him is custom made, and for all seasons of life. With Jesus, I feel good, feel right, and feel safe. And the best part of all, I'll have Him forever.

Jesus is a **comfortable** person . . . therefore I feel unthreatened with Him as a friend.

He is the Rock, his works are perfect, and all his ways are just.
A faithful God who does no wrong, upright and just is he.
Deuteronomy 32:4

No One Else Could Ever Fill His Shoes

Jesus is like "an old shoe." He has that certain "comfort" factor about him that attracts people easily. We see this early in the Gospel accounts as he began building relationships with those who became his disciples. When Jesus invited them to follow him, they responded immediately. No awkward hesitation. No polite excuses. No "I'll pray about it and get back to you" stuff. They just up and left their fishing boats and tax collecting booths. That's pretty amazing! In Matthew 8:19, a teacher of the law tells Jesus, " . . . *I will follow you wherever you go.*" What an extravagant promise to make! He wanted to be wherever Jesus was. What prompts that kind of commitment, that kind of relational zeal?

Have you ever been away from home and met someone you were instantly attracted to? Did you inquire about where that person lived? Perhaps a little voice in your mind was saying, "I hope it's near me 'cause I want to hang out with you again and again, and get to know you better. I'd like to have you as a friend."

Jesus is the master of comfort, of sensitivity. He has *sechul* (a Jewish term meaning *wisdom*) enabling Him to deal sensitively with people. It takes wisdom to handle people with skill. I made a careful study in Scripture watching for situations where Jesus dealt sensitively with people. This Jesus, this one who is too kind to ever be cruel, had different ways of dealing with people. The circumstances or problems they were experiencing were often the same (or very similar), yet He had no standard "one size fits all" response to them. This surprised me. It hardly seemed like an *efficient* approach for one whose mission was to bring Good News to the world.

The Lord ministers in different ways in the lives of those with similar problems. Why? Jesus has the wisdom to see beyond the problem to the person. With *sensitivity* to each person's unique personality and needs, He responds uniquely despite the sameness of their circumstances. See the box below to witness just a few examples:

Jesus brought conversion differently to people.

1. *Jesus called Zacchaeus down from a tree. "I must stay at your house today," Jesus said to the little man with a very big problem. He could've brought him to salvation publicly. But he didn't.*
   Luke 19:2–9
2. *Yet another time, we meet a sorry, sobbing sinner at Simon the Pharisee's home, and she was forgiven and accepted very publicly.*
   Luke 7:36

Jesus brought sight to the blind differently.

1. The Master touched blind eyes to heal.
   Matthew 9:27–30
2. He spit on blind eyes to heal and put His hands on him.
   Mark 8:23
3. He simply spoke the healing, saying to the blind man "Go thy way, thy faith hath made thee whole."
   Mark 10:52 (KJV)

He dealt differently with two non-Jewish people.

1. Before making her daughter whole, Jesus first ignored, then refused, then appeared to deride a Canaanite woman who had come to Him.
   Matthew 15:22–28
2. He voluntarily, willingly made a Roman Centurion's servant whole.
   Matthew 8:5–15

Jesus spoke to would-be followers and directed them in different ways.

1. A healed demoniac begged to go with Jesus but was told to go home to his family.
   Mark 5:18–19
2. Jesus instructed two men not to go home, even to say good-bye to family, or attend to a father's burial.
   Luke 9:59–62
3. Jesus told a rich young ruler to go sell everything and give to the poor, and then come follow Him
   Luke 18:22

Since methods of handling situations may differ because of the person involved, we need to be sensitive to the Holy Spirit if we are going to be sensitive readers of the souls of men. This involves seeking after God's wisdom in each of our relationships, identifying individual needs, and responding accordingly.

Now, at times Jesus appears to be *insensitive* to people. The Canaanite woman mentioned earlier seems to be dealt with harshly. Jesus' own mother and brothers appear to receive an insensitive response from Him in the following account:

> *While Jesus was still talking to the crowd, his mother and brothers stood outside, wanting to speak to him. Someone told him, "Your mother and brothers are standing outside, wanting to speak to you." He replied to him, "Who is my mother, and who are my brothers?" Pointing to his disciples, he said, "Here are my mother and my brothers. For whoever does the will of my Father in heaven is my brother and sister and mother."*
> *Matthew 12:50*

What appears to be insensitivity on Jesus' part is, in reality, love for individuals. In addition, the Lord has higher purposes in mind than what appears on the surface. He desires to test the Canaanite woman's faith as gold. He uses the situation with his mother and brothers above as a teachable moment to instruct on the preeminence of a spiritual relationship to God over family and others. He is not proposing rejection of one's mother. He's saying:

> *Love the Lord your God with all your heart and with all your soul and with all your mind.*
> *Matthew 22:37*

> *Anyone who comes to me but refuses to let go of father, mother, spouse,*
> *children, brothers, sisters—yes, even one's own self!—can't be my disciple.*
> *Luke 14:26 (The Message Bible)*

He consistently demonstrates sensitivity by being people-centered, not position-centered:

> *Your attitude should be the same as that of Christ Jesus: Who, being in very*
> *nature God, did not consider equality with God something to be grasped, but*
> *made himself nothing, taking the very nature of a servant, being made in*
> *human likeness. And being found in appearance as a man, he humbled*
> *himself and became obedient to death—even death on a cross!*
> *Philippians 2:5–8*

The following is an example to try, just try, to give you a picture of the transcendent sensitivity of Jesus Christ. It is the classic story of *The Princess and the Pea,* an enchanting tale of the search by a royal family for a princess bride suitable for their son, the prince.

> *Under 10 fluffy, feathery mattresses, the queen mother placed a lowly,*
> *lonely pea—just an itsy-bitsy near-weightless ball. Women near and far*
> *declared they were princesses in order to gain favor.*
> *The ingenuity of the test was to invite each bridal candidate in turn to*
> *sleep on the top mattress for one night. The following morning the queen*
> *would ask, "How did you sleep?"*
> *"Splendidly!" was always the answer from each impostor.*
> *Then one day, the reply quietly came from a lovely girl, "I am so sorry.*
> *This is difficult for me to confess, but I didn't sleep a wink. I tossed and*
> *turned all night."*

At that confession the royal family realized they had a real princess in this maiden. For surely only a real princess would be sensitive enough to be kept awake by the pea! She and the prince were married because it was her sensitivity that had won the love of the prince and his family.

Of course, it seems *impossible* in the natural realm to be so sensitive that you could sleep atop such a tower of mattresses and be alert to a pea beneath the bottom one.

(If it were my biscuits or my brownies . . . I could understand. Even my gravy is lumpy enough to feel through ten mattresses!) But this exquisite, fine-tuned sense of "perceiving" is what Jesus possesses. And it is what goes into making a person "sensitive" to other's feelings, situations, needs, anxieties, insecurities, and "tender spots."

Spiritually speaking, we want to be "sensitive" like the real princess. To be able to sense the needs of others, to discern their comfort or lack of it, their pain or their joy, their pretending or honesty, their spiritual hunger or disinterest.

The Bible teaches that God intends to remake us in the image of His Son Jesus—the Perfect Shoe. Jesus longs for us to become sensitive, that we might be effective messengers of His Word. How will He accomplish this?

From the moment we become His appointed messengers, our feet become His property. The Lord fits them with Himself. Our shameful feet shod with calluses, corns, bunions, and more, no longer need to be hidden. Those feet that may have kicked others hard and wounded shins are free to be bare.

Only the Lord *gives* you (through grace) new feet and only the Lord adorns those feet perfectly. In order to have new feet (a metaphor for a new heart/spirit), you must repent of all the kicking against God's commands. Hold out your broken feet to Jesus Christ and ask Him to do a miracle of recreation and to wash your feet through the blood that poured out of Him at the Cross. In doing this, He releases you from the bondage of condemnation. He replaces those worn out feet with shoutin', dancin' feet that are pointed only to His glory and to a new eternity—Heaven.

With full knowledge of the condition of your feet at all times (your spiritual "walk" gives it away!), He brings about the necessary changes (sanctification) to produce the desired end result—beautiful feet!

> *How beautiful on the mountains*
> *are the **feet** of those who bring good news,*
> *who proclaim peace,*
> *who bring good tidings,*
> *who proclaim salvation,*
> *who say to Zion,*
> *"Your God reigns!"*
> *Isaiah 52:7 (emphasis mine)*

I Think That I Shall Never View A Thing As Lovely As A Shoe

I Can Deal with Anything if I Have the Right Shoes

"A woman can't have too many shoes or too many friends."

I know a woman who has not only heard this saying, she abides in it. This shoe-loving lady was a fellow conference speaker years ago. Having unpacked my two pairs of shoes, black Naturalizers and taupe Easy Spirits, I went to her hotel room. There before me was one of the long walls lined with *fifteen* pairs of shoes . . . for a weekend conference! Varied colors, heel sizes, closed toe, open toe . . . and that's not including bedroom slippers and flip-flops. I had heard about "shoe people" but this was my first bona fide encounter. I thought to myself, *I don't understand this woman. Why in the world would she resort to this parade of shoes? What must she have left at home? Oy Vey! I bet her guestroom has become a warehouse!*

I ought to be careful when I begin to judge others, for I may be judged in the same way. Not about my shoes, though perhaps about my friends. I have them lined up all across the country—all "Naturalizers" and "Easy Spirits"—but in varied colors and sizes. I regularly hear myself extolling the wonders of this friend to that friend. And I say to all of them, "When we get to heaven, I'm opening a delicatessen where you'll all meet and experience each other's wonders . . . and slurp Matzoh Ball soup."

I recall the day when I lunged into my closet to reorganize my shoes. Looking at each shoe, I identified qualities in them that resembled a cherished friend. Each pair had a different style and performed a distinct function in my life. I wore them to different places. I needed them under various conditions.

The people I most wanted around me were welcoming right from the start. Loving, kind, patient . . . oh, how I needed that. Every one of these friends continues to be a sensitive person, considering the needs of others before her own, which translates into being *comfortable.* I am crazy over friends (and shoes) like that!

Though I highly esteem their talents, if these people weren't *first* easy to know and comfortable to "wear," I'd never have developed a deeper relationship with them. Like trying on a pair of attractive but uncomfortable shoes in the store, I'd pass them back to the salesclerk with a polite but certain, "No thanks. They just don't feel right."

♫ "These Are a Few of My Favorite Things" ♫ Shoes . . . and Friends

Do you ever think about your favorite things? The songstress singing "My Favorite Things" lists "whiskers on kittens and warm woolen mittens." Two of my favorite things, as you now know, are comfortable shoes and comfortable friends.

Whether it's a sole for your feet or a soul for your heart, the comfort they provide is invaluable. Pretend you're standing just a *few feet* away from my closet. I'm going to let you have a look at my shoes, and some of my most sensitive, comfortable friends. The soul of the matter is the manner of their comfort, so from sneaker to slipper, it's on with the show, as they say. Or should it be . . . *now, on with the shoe. There's no business like shoe business!*

The Travel Sneaker

I have a soft leather pair of tennis shoes that are half the size in bulk of the usual type. They weigh less and have no hard rubber protection, almost like ballet slippers, but with shoelaces. This is my travel pair of sneakers. Because they fit my baggage well, I can take them anywhere. They are extremely *flexible,* with *much give* to them. I'm able to fold them in half and stuff them in any spare luggage space. When I unpack, these shoes *bounce back* to their original shape.

I use these same characteristics to describe my long-standing friend Pat Rawlings from Virginia. In a short period of time, my close friend walked with me through the illness and death of my husband, the death of my stepfather, and the severe mental illness of my mother. She also saw me through a ruptured artery which nearly cost me my life and a relationship which nearly devoured me.

At first my friend was crushed and compressed by so much hard news within a short span, but like the squashed shoes in the luggage, she bounced back to her original shape. Pat endured much *wear and tear* sharing in my traumas. She never actually fainted over any of them . . . but I did hear her go silent over the phone a few times . . . *are you there, Pat?*

Pert, perky Pat willingly allows herself to be lovingly tucked into my overstuffed emotional baggage full of terror, confusion, hurt, temptation, and more!

*Pat is a comfortable friend . . . and a **faithful** friend.*

When you pass through the waters,
I will be with you;
and when you pass through the rivers,
they will not sweep over you.
When you walk through the fire,
you will not be burned;
the flames will not set you ablaze.
Isaiah 43:2

But Ruth replied, "Don't urge me to leave you or to turn back from you.
Where you go I will go, and where you stay I will stay."
Ruth 1:16

The Walking Shoe

There's another pair of tennis shoes in my closet. They are monsters compared with the travel pair. They are meant for the huge metal contraption in my bedroom. I hear a gasp from one reader . . . "Oh, no! It's the fiend! It's the taskmaster!" Yes, it's the treadmill . . . better known as the "dreadmill." *Groan.* My treadmill shoes can actually speak to me! (All the others in my closet are mute.) This pair insists, "You must exercise! That's an expensive piece of equipment out there. Get your money's worth. Besides, you need bone density, you need cardiac stimulation, you need limbering up."

Donna Arthur from Pennsylvania is my comfortable friend who stimulates me to *exercise my spiritual senses.* What a valuable friend she has been for years. She causes me to *stretch* myself spiritually, to *reach* higher, and to *press* harder in pursuit of the knowledge of God. Our relationship began when she was assigned to edit my first book, *Feelings Women Rarely Share.* Donna was easy to work with, but the subject matter in the book was not. I love having someone as a close, close friend who constantly *lifts up* the Lord, *grasps* the deep wonders of His Word, and *pumps up* others to do the same. She challenges and encourages me, causes me to think, and spurs me on to *grow stronger* in the Lord.

*Donna is a comfortable friend . . . and a **strengthening** friend.*

. . . those who hope in the Lord
will renew their strength.
They will soar on wings like eagles;
they will run and not grow weary,
they will walk and not be faint.
Isaiah 40:31

. . . I beat my body and make it my slave so that after I have preached to others, I myself will not be disqualified for the prize.
1 Corinthians 9:27

The Oldie but Goodie Shoe

I'll never be able to replace my all-time favorite pair of "tennies." I don't wear them in public, though I wear them daily when I'm indoors alone. They would be an eyesore to anyone but me. They are grubby, scuffed gray at the toe, and the bottoms have lost their tread.

What is it about this shoe that has so endeared itself to me? It is a broken shoe, "broken in" to its limit. When it was new and played outdoors, it went through rain (and shrank a bit), mud (and got messed up), and wet grass (and was stained). Now the shoe stays indoors and is very forgiving of me *sans* makeup and hairstyle. The shoe has paced with me for miles of praying and cleaning bathrooms and making beds. It has been on the floor with me as I have pounded my fists, kicked my feet, and cried. These shoes are definitely keepers!

My close friend, Barbie Eslin from Florida is like a "broken in" shoe. My buddy has been through many trials of all sorts, and then, some years ago, she became severely physically afflicted, even despairing of life at times. Because of her past, she is a broken vessel; the empathy that oozes from her is a priceless treasure to have in a friend. She *feels* with me. She *understands* and *accepts* the private me. I know when I talk with her of my broken dreams or my angst over tribulations which play like background music in my life, this is the friend who, tried and tested herself, can relate deeply and can easily weep with me. *Barbie* is a keeper![2]

*Barbie is a comfortable friend . . . and an **empathetic** friend.*

The sacrifices of God are a broken spirit;
a broken and contrite heart,
O God, you will not despise.
Psalm 51:17

Praise be to the God and Father of our Lord Jesus Christ, the Father of
compassion and the God of all comfort, who comforts us in all our troubles,
so that we can comfort those in any trouble with the comfort we ourselves
have received from God.
2 Corinthians 1:3–4

---

[2] (P.S. Recently an amazing breakthrough has occurred and she has relief that is enough to set her feet a dancin'!)

The Anti-Gravity Shoe

Bounce! That's what my new bedroom slippers do. These are called "anti-gravity shoes" by Easy Spirit. They're *funny* shoes and make you feel like you're walking on air. In fact, I'd say they *lift me up,* "Whoosh, poof, *an' a* whoosh, poof." I've never been able to conquer a pogo stick. Yet, that's the kind of "jump up and be happy" sensation I get when I wear these. It's the air in the soles that enables them to give me a lift as I pad around.

I'm certain it's not hot air filling up and pouring out of Donna Alberta of Michigan. It is the joy of the Lord! That is her strength. You feel like you're tripping the light fantastic when with her. Lighthearted and fun, yet heavy with intelligence and an appreciation of her wonder-working God, she is *too* delightful. She is the best! Joy, joy, joy exudes from her. Her patter is insightful and uplifting. The '50s "Song of the South" movie gave us the melody "Zippity Doo Da." That song title captures her spirit well.

Once when I deplaned in Detroit, Donna was there to meet me. Jubilant and bouncy, she grabbed me in front of all and hugged and hugged and shouted with joy that I was there. We had fun even getting to the baggage claim area as she grabbed me to peer through holes in canvas curtains hiding some "in the works" refurbishments. We jingled out the door, mingled at a restaurant, tingled at a vitamin store, and giggled at her thrift store purchases from that morning.

Her wisdom, insight, and laughter have guided me through preparing this book. In my Atlanta condo, we were connected at the hip (a *broad* generality) as we prayerfully sought the Lord to change the adage of "Clothes Make the Man" to "Shoes Make the Woman." We laughed, we interrupted, we ate, we worshipped, we worked . . . all to the tune of "I've Grown Accustomed to Your Face." (Or rather, "I've Grown Accustomed to Your Face without Foundation.")

*Donna is a comfortable friend . . . and a **joyful**, **uplifting** friend.*

Be joyful always; pray continually; give thanks in all circumstances,
for this is God's will for you in Christ Jesus.
1 Thessalonians 5:16–18

But may the righteous be glad and rejoice before God;
may they be happy and joyful.
Psalm 68:3

Let love and faithfulness never leave you;
bind them around your neck,
write them on the tablet of your heart.
Then you will win favor and a good name in the sight of
God and man.
Proverbs 3:3–4

The Slide

Ah, the slides. They're the latest style of shoe this year. (And maybe for years to come because of their slip-on ease and comfort when wearing.) Anyone who sports slides may lift up her head and not be ashamed to proclaim, "I am up-to-date."

Being alert to the current fashion scene is one thing. It might help you *look* sharp and be "*with it.*" But, how much more fortunate to be alert to the times, catching the fresh winds of the Spirit, sensing anew what God is saying to the church today. That's what helps you *be* sharp and be "with *Him*" wherever He's leading.

A precious gift of a friend is Lorri Elliott of Georgia. She is a consummate reader. The bookstore is a favorite hangout for this *fresh manna* friend. On the other hand, I, the wandering Jew, travel around the nation teaching, leaving me no time to sip a *latte* at bookstores, perusing the latest bendings, mendings, and trendings in the Christian world.

Whenever Lorri and I converse, she brings me up-to-date with her talk of great books. Not with the dreary, "same old, same old" worldly news and views. Instead, she nourishes my hungry soul with the latest "sensings" of how and where God is at work. I eat much more than an egg salad sandwich when with Lorri. I eat and drink of the Spirit.

*Lorri is a comfortable friend . . . and a **nourishing** friend.*

As iron sharpens iron, so one man sharpens another.
Proverbs 27:17

Since we live by the Spirit, let us keep in step with the Spirit.
Galatians 5:25

The Thermal Slipper

I regularly experience notoriously cold feet (unrelated to my public speaking), so I have a love affair going with my thermal, boot-like, black slippers. Oh, that I could have these foot-furnaces at my disposal at all times.

Can you imagine how "at home" my feet are in a slipper meant for Eskimos? A slipper so thick when worn that I appear to have huge casts, painted black on both feet. Oh, the treasure of a friend who makes you feel "at home"— who, when you arrive at her doorstep, tired and chilled by the demands of living, totally envelops you with her warmth and hospitality.

That is Kay Donovan from Michigan. She is my daughter Jill's mother-in-law. When Kay gets a hold of me, warmth is all I experience. I am treated as if I have just emerged from a frozen meat locker. I am wrapped in a blanket of love that includes gourmet food, gourmet old movies, gourmet malt balls, and to-die-for milk shakes from the soda fountain in her '50s decorated basement. The attitude Kay and her dear hubby Terry show is "We're here to serve you, you tired Jewish American Princess." By the time I leave, I am simmering nicely inside, all the way down to my feet, and am ready to go back to icy Atlanta. (Well, don't you think fifty-four degrees in the winter is *really* cold??)

*Kay is a comfortable friend . . . and a **warm, welcoming** friend.*

Offer hospitality to one another without grumbling.
1 Peter 4:9

. . . and you will receive a rich welcome into the eternal kingdom
of our Lord and Savior Jesus Christ.
2 Peter 1:11

The Faux Foot Slipper

There is one purposely comical pair of slippers in my possession. They are tight fitting and shaped exactly like human feet. The entire cotton slipper is painted as an anatomically correct foot. Even on the bottom. When you wear these they appear, from a distance, to be one's actual feet. The slippers do a marvelous job covering up calluses and bunions . . . a perfect camouflage. In other words, they make ugly feet look really swell . . . though when you see them up close, their cover-up job is discovered and they bring on gales of laughter.

Mary Ann Faint from Georgia is my superb friend who has known me longer than any of the others. We've known each other before the foundation of our faith and before our children were born. She and I were neighbors in Baltimore, and she became my secretary when I began to travel in ministry.

The information she has in her head, as a very close friend and as someone who did all my mail, is locked in her brain vault. There is no doubt that this trusted friend makes me look good anytime my name comes up. What a cover I have in her! She has seen my "ugly feet" with all their bunions and calluses (my struggles with people and circumstances of all sorts), yet she paints a picture of me as a glorious foot over any fungal development from the past. I imagine if anyone ever gossiped unkindly about me, Mary Ann would blurt out, "My foot! Judy hung the moon!"

*Mary Ann is a comfortable friend . . . and a **shielding** friend.*

Above all, love each other deeply, because love covers over a multitude of sins.
1 Peter 4:8

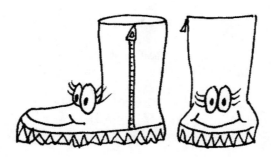

The Ski Boot

Last year, my après-ski boots worked to keep me from falling on the après (French for "after") part of my body. I was in Beaver Creek, Colorado, for a week on my own. For someone no longer skiing, these all-terrain wonders with the treads are "the" shoe of choice at a ski resort. They are to the foot what the snow tire is to the car. They see you through when the going gets rough, and they help you keep your traction.

Being "solo" in this snowy setting meant there was no one to steady me when I'd start to slip and slide. These boots were made not only for walkin', but also for climbing up snowbanks and getting down mountains with no skis. These dependable boots helped me slog my way through the tough-to-navigate places that brought me up to awesome, inspiring mountain views. They never went out from under me as I made my way cautiously back down the imposing slopes. They led me triumphantly into the lodge, where a blazing fireplace awaited the skiers, who compare "mountain" notes, cocoa in hand. (I am not a ski bunny, but a snowflake—I love the snow more than any other condition in nature, so I delight in any conversation about snow.)

My friend Jeanne Lyles from Florida has been there for me in the lonely, cold times—when the dark night of the soul drove me to the mountaintop to pray and seek God's face. Like those who held up Moses' arms to beseech the Lord's favor in the midst of the battle, Jeanne lent me her strength. When my journey seemed like an impossible trek up a slippery, icy slope, she gave me spiritual traction to stay the course.

*Jeanne is a comfortable friend . . . and a **steadying** friend.*

And Saul's son Jonathan went to David . . .
and helped him find strength in God.
1 Samuel 23:16

My intercessor is my friend as my eyes pour out tears to God;
on behalf of a man he pleads with God as a man pleads for his friend.
Job 16:20–21

A kindhearted woman gains respect,
but ruthless men gain only wealth.
Proverbs 11:16

The Loafer

When I was growing up in Philadelphia, every girl—I mean *every* girl—had penny loafers. No other shoe on the market was as comfortable in my teenage years (sneakers were strictly for gym at school back then), and we all had a penny inserted in a small slit on the top of the shoe. The loafer was a relaxed shoe, well deserving its name.

Bobbie Wilkinson hails from Virginia (near Washington, D.C.) Her imaginative illustrations bring this book to life with their playful animation. And is she ever a sight for sore feet! Her welcoming smile and arms bid you to kick off both your shoes and your cares, kick back, and loaf around a while.

Bobbie and her husband Tom, for years a senior editor with the Washington Post, live in a huge three-level barn which is so phenomenal in concept it should be featured in one of those "homes" magazines. Her unique home warms the heart, much like an inviting foot-stomping country hoedown.

To experience Bobbie is to experience life, love, and laughter. Bobbie is the kind of close friend who will be the last to board an elevator with me, and face backwards in front of fifteen puzzled and judging pairs of eyes, as if our behavior is the norm. She and I are usually seen doubled over. All the loosey-goosey Bobbie needs is a penny between her lips and she'd be a dead ringer for the '50s penny loafer. I go-fer loafers. We all could use this shoe in our lives.

*Bobbie is a comfortable friend . . . and a **fun, relaxing** friend.*

A cheerful heart is good medicine,
but a crushed spirit dries up the bones.
Proverbs 17:22

. . . he who refreshes others will himself be refreshed.
Proverbs 11:25

The Transparent Shoe

Popular this season is the shoe that is transparent. It humbly croaks out, "I got nuttin' to hide." What a terrific idea for a shoe! I can wear it with any color. It enables me to pack my leopard dress with Zebra scarf (just kidding) and add to the luggage my orange pantsuit with pink polka dot collar and cuffs (not kidding) with just one pair of shoes, the "see-through" pair. These shoes differ from all the opaque shoes—as one can see right through them.

If you ever want transparency in something other than a shoe, go to Florida, where Jo Anderson lets it all hang out. She is real, direct, and honest, if nothing else. Jo wears no mask as a friend. Her honesty helps me to take off *my* mask. I feel life principles are better *caught* than taught. When you're around a giving person, you find yourself reaching for your wallet more to help others. When you're around a no-pretense person, it is easier to reveal the truth about your failings. I've always benefited from the hours we've spent together because I taste the benefits of authenticity. Making it wonderfully easy to be yourself when you're around her, Jo is not even tempted to perform. She offers no apologies but says, "Hey, this is me. What you see is what you get."

*Jo is a comfortable friend . . . and a **transparent** friend.*

When Jesus saw Nathaniel approaching, he said of him,
"Here is a true Israelite, in whom there is nothing false."
John 1:47

An honest answer is like a kiss on the lips.
Proverbs 24:26

The Sandal

Atlanta (also called "Hotlanta") affords numerous days to wear my Birkenstock sandals. Most of you probably have sandals . . . and don't you just love them? There is one downside, however. The exposure of the foot makes it easy to experience scrapes and stubs, which translate into pain. If I can, I'll avoid pain at all cost! When wearing sandals, I'm a little more careful on cement steps and dandelion patches loaded with yellow jackets. Would you wear sandals in the snake-infested Brazilian forests? Sandals make you terribly vulnerable.

I like sandal friends, though. I need a friend like Doris Gamble from Mississippi. She has had much pain in the past and is a person who is sensitive to someone's "hot buttons." She is careful not to push those buttons—the places where you've been wounded before, an irrational fear or two you may have. Oh, how I love Doris who understands my tender-footedness. There is an understanding between sandal friends: "I've been hurt myself and it's pretty awful, so I won't go there unless you ask me to." This friend is careful not to step on toes and is sensitive to Achilles' heels. A sandal friend is aware of "Do unto others. . . ." They don't take advantage of the exposed toes and admonish: "Get a life!"

*Doris is a comfortable friend . . . and an **understanding** friend.*

This is what the Lord Almighty says: "Administer true justice;
show mercy and compassion to one another."
Zechariah 7:9

Therefore, as God's chosen people, holy and dearly loved, clothe yourselves
with compassion, kindness, humility, gentleness and patience.
Colossians 3:12

The Classic Pump

My basic black pump goes with almost anything. It's always there at my beck and call, a must-have shoe. It just won't quit or go out of style. I never fail to see someone (with good taste too) wearing the classic pump, no matter what the fashion world is doing with our feet.

My dependable "basic" is ready to go anyplace, blending with almost everything I wear. No matter if it's a wedding or a school bazaar the shoe never says, "No, you mustn't don me today. I just don't fit in that situation."

Delores Nance of Georgia never fails me. Like the classic pump, she is an all-occasion friend. Whatever I need her for, she is always willing to serve. This petite friend has tremendous fashion sense and helps me select suitable apparel for ministry; she marvelously rearranges furniture, hangs pictures, and bakes for me. She volunteers her "fun" husband Ron to repair anything that breaks, and to uncrash my computer. The girl can do anything! I'd ask her to marry me, but Ron stands in the way!

Most importantly, Delores is ready at the drop of a hat to drive me anyplace, or to fly anywhere to assist me. She's been in the trenches in Florida with me for my ailing mother and on the benches of churches with me to help at conferences.

She is that basic friend who is there for all seasons. I have never seen a person who so unobtrusively blends with any situation I invite her to be a part of. She is ready, willing, and able for anything and for all the times of my life.

Delores is a comfortable friend . . . and a **dependable** *friend.*

. . . because God has said, "Never will I leave you; never will I forsake you."
So we say with confidence, "The Lord is my helper;
I will not be afraid. What can man do to me?"
Hebrews 13:5–6

The purposes of a man's heart are deep waters,
but a man of understanding draws them out.
Proverbs 20:5

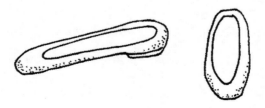

The Gold Flat

I really like my gold flat. It's not a shiny gold, but a quiet, subdued bronzy gold. It blends well with brown pieces. Browns are difficult to match. The gold shoe quietly and simply says to the pleated brown skirt, "I'm here for you."

It is said, "Silence is golden." Oh, to have a friend who can keep quiet and give you "your moment." Verna Clemmer from Pennsylvania listens and listens without yawning. Verna encourages me to share my heart and truly wants to listen, so she may know how to pray. What a gift to me when she gives me the luxury of talking freely and at long length, if need be. She never rushes me. What a sounding board who never suggests my "sounding off" is boring.

When the cares of this sad world overwhelm my mind, when concerns for those I love pierce my heart, when life's problems seem to loom larger than the God I lean on, I need a patient listener, someone who will allow me to unload my burdens. Just airing my anxieties with someone who won't feel compelled to give me instant "answers" is sweet relief to my soul.

Job described his friends as, "Miserable comforters!" Why? They spouted reasons, remedies, and religious platitudes in response to his writhing pain. All he wanted was the soothing balm of silent lips and listening ears.

*Verna is a comfortable friend . . . and a **listening** friend.*

Those who listen carefully to others are in the best position for hearing the Great Other.

—David Adam[3]

My dear brothers, take note of this:
Everyone should be quick to listen, slow to speak . . .
James 1:19

---

[3] David Adam, "The Eye of the Eagle," Christianity Today, May 22, 2000

The Sturdy Shoe

When my parents began to notice I was pigeon-toed (toes turn in when walking), they took me to Samuel's Shoe Store, a children's footwear shop with an x-ray machine that shone a green light on one's feet for measurement purposes. It was fun to see my green feet, but I turned pale when, as a ten-year-old, I heard Mr. Samuel Cohen tell my mother and father, "She needs an oxford. An orthopedic shoe is called for."

Yeeks! My life is over! Everyone's wearing penny loafers. I'll lose my standing!

"No, you will be able to stand straight . . . with your toes not pointing at each other," said the wise Mr. Cohen.

For a few years I had to wear brown orthopedic shoes. Because they kept me foundationally foot-perfect, I am no longer pigeon-toed. And guess what? In my closet today is a pair of brown chunky-heeled pumps. They're not delicate and flattering but they allow me to almost skip through the busiest airport in the world (which happens to be located in Atlanta). Navigating the concourses and trams is no easy *feat*.

This sturdy shoe also allows me to take a solid stance for sometimes two or three hours of being up on my feet at a meeting. (For the record, that's ten minutes of teaching and the rest of the time eating at a banquet table stashed with brownies, lemon squares, spinach dip, and chunks of cheese.)

Glenna Salsbury of Arizona is planted firmly in the absolutes of the faith. This child of God is not one to waiver. She inspires those around her to stay securely rooted to foundational biblical doctrine. Glenna, a former president of the National Speaker's Association, has spoken in corporate America for many years. I first heard her in that venue, where there were a lot of professionally pigeon-toed, flat-footed people taking notes. She fitted them with some business orthopedics. But more importantly, she consistently modeled the benefit of walking with Jesus.

Engraved on her heart is the Word of God, and this is obvious whether she is shining brightly in front of an AT&T audience or a church group. The Amplified Bible uses the words "stable" and "stability" often, and that is what Glenna embodies. I am thrilled to have this *sturdy* friend who keeps me focused on the *basics* of Christianity, rejecting current trends and embracing the historic essentials of the faith.

*Glenna is a comfortable friend . . . and a **stable** friend.*

Watch your life and doctrine closely . . .
1 Timothy 4:16

My steps have held to your paths; my feet have not slipped.
Psalm 17:5

The Ruby Slippers

"There's no place like home," Dorothy pined as she clicked the heels of her magical shoes together three times, reciting with each click her heart's desire. Decades ago I gazed at those enchanted ruby slippers on Judy Garland's feet in *The Wizard of Oz*—I never forgot them. They went far beyond any other shoes I had ever seen! As a youngster I wished such sparkling red sequined footwear could adorn my feet. Instead, the dull brown oxfords remained my daily fare.

A couple of years back, I was browsing in a shoe store when my heart skipped a beat. There sat a pair of ruby slippers on display!! They were size 7. Not too far off from my size 8½. The problem was they were a children's size 7. So what? In minutes, they were mine. I can't wear them on my feet of course, but they are useful to my soul. Those dainty, little shoes keep the prospect of *Sunday's a comin'* before me!

If you ever need a friend to remind you of eternity, to remind you of what awaits God's children, to help you get your eyes off the things of the earth, it is Marian Kough in Florida. Whenever we are together we *click shoes* on this. She and I are longing for Jesus to come back to take us to our Home faraway. It is marvelous to have a friend who encourages you to allow the things of earth to grow strangely dim.

For many years I have surveyed believers, asking them "How often do you think about Heaven?" Reporting on an ascending scale of one to ten, most said "four" or "five." I have been a *perfect ten* from the beginning of my relationship with the Lord. Marian and I discovered we are alike in our excitement of what God has prepared for those who love Him. There are not many I know who actually enjoy growing older. We do. Each birthday brings us one year closer to going to our eternal Home. Maybe you can see why it is so good for me to have her in my life. Besides, she is just too marvelous for words as a servant of the Lord down here on Earth.

*Marian is a comfortable friend . . . and a **heavenly-minded** friend.*

As it is written:
"No eye has seen, no ear has heard, no mind has conceived
what God has prepared for those who love him"
1 Corinthians 2:9

In my Father's house are many rooms; if it were not so, I would have told
you. I am going there to prepare a place for you.
John 14:2

The Designer Shoe

The next shoe is *not* in my closet. None of my present shoes are pricey. I don't own a single "name-dropper" shoe. Yet I yearn to own just one pair of Ferragamos. Those who can buy just about any shoe on the market know the name Ferragamo. The sterling reputation of the shoe is its biggest asset. It is a quality shoe worth having.

A couple of years ago, I was a presenter at a conference with Joni Eareckson Tada, the world-renown Christian speaker. When her name is mentioned, the hearer envisions a woman in a wheelchair. But more than that, there is a priceless, Ferragamo-like *persona* about her that speaks of quality and integrity. Elizabeth Elliott, Catherine Marshall, Corrie Ten Boom—these are names that also denote inestimable quality and integrity. They have served as distinguished ambassadors of the Lord Jesus. Like Ferragamo shoes, it's not easy to replicate them.

Interestingly, when I was standing near Joni, I noticed she was wearing *Ferragamo* shoes. These shoes were never used other than to envelop her feet.

Why have them if you are virtually crippled and unable to walk? Because *first of all* a Ferragamo is a comfortable shoe. Joni may not have any feeling in her feet, but the shoes she wears must not rub, pinch, or threaten her disused feet. She can't afford sores so she wisely has chosen to afford a shoe with an undisputed reputation for extraordinary comfort and fit. That is why it can command such a high price.

I have a Ferragamo person in my life. He is priceless to me! Ferragamo may be the priciest footwear in a shoe closet, but Pat Boone, my Hollywood teenage idol whose fame at one time surpassed Elvis Presley's, is the most valuable person in my *life closet.* His worth is in the millions to the record, film, and TV industries. Pat's past yearly performances at the Fremont Hotel in Las Vegas garnered large revenues for all concerned. But his value *to me* far exceeds all of those worldly acclaims combined. In fact, it is infinite, immeasurable, incalculable.

He is the most priceless friend in my life because he introduced me to the Messiah decades ago. Because of *his* sterling reputation, I appeared to be of great worth when Pat walked into the lobby of Caesar's Palace (Las Vegas) and ushered me out on his arm, assisting me into his car for my water baptism appointment. His reflected worth shone on me to onlookers. To know and be known by *the* Pat Boone made me feel like a million dollars. It may be a heady thing to be discipled by such a prestigious performer, but what has kept me in touch with him is the fact that Pat is one of the most comfortably safe people I have ever met.

*Pat is a comfortable friend . . . and a **priceless** friend.*

How priceless is your unfailing love!
Psalm 36:7

The New Kid Shoes on the Block

There was an old woman who lived in a shoe. She had so many shoes, she didn't know what to do!

So, she acquired them all. She sure did. This elderly woman (an acquaintance's mother) was mentally ill and had gone to a mall to spend much money . . . on shoes. The leather *kid* shoes were never worn and were my size. Eventually, they fell into my hands; subsequently three comfortable pairs fell onto my feet. I would have never *bought them.* These additions to my closet would cause me to say, "What gifts, Lord. When I had no time to shop nor money to spare, You provided new shoes." The Lord knew my need.

Moving to Atlanta several years ago was a bit traumatic. There was no base of friends here. Along came three women from diverse suburbs, each of whom chased me until I *caught them!*

If they hadn't persevered with cords of loving phone calls, chocolates(!), and the like (even an invitation to a daughter's wedding, though I was a stranger!), I would never have taken notice of them. The Atlanta girls had an uncanny sense that "Judy and I were meant to be close friends." Just as I have little time to shop, I have less time to develop new friendships. Now I say, "What gifts, Lord. When I had no time to shop *for friends,* You provided new ones." The Lord knew my need . . . in Atlanta.

Sandy Feit, Bev O'Brien, and Maryann LaFera are comfortable friends . . .
*and **persevering** friends.*

We love him, because he first loved us.
1 John 4:19 KJV

*While Peter thought on the vision, the Spirit said unto him, "Behold, **three men seek thee**. Arise therefore, and get thee down, and go with them, doubting nothing: **for I have sent them.**"*
Acts 10:19–20 KJV (emphasis mine)

A Comfortable Soul Is the Way to Go!

When listing all the shoes that were stand-ins for real friends, it is obvious the talents and personalities vary extremely. The list below is a reminder of a multifaceted, wonderful God.

THE TRAVEL SNEAKER
THE WALKING SHOE
THE OLDIE BUT GOODIE
THE ANTI-GRAVITY SHOE
THE SLIDE
THE THERMAL SLIPPER
THE FAUX FOOT SLIPPER
THE SKI BOOT
THE LOAFER

THE TRANSPARENT SHOE
THE SANDAL
THE CLASSIC PUMP
THE GOLD FLAT
THE STURDY SHOE
THE RUBY SLIPPERS
THE DESIGNER SHOE
THE NEW KID SHOES ON THE BLOCK

What they hold in common reminds me most of Jesus. And that is—they are well-heeled with His *sensitive* manner. And though all these shoes are comfortable and have their own separate values, there is only One who perfectly holds all these qualities at all times—*faithful, strengthening, empathetic, joyful, uplifting, nourishing, warm, welcoming, shielding, steadying, fun, relaxing, transparent, understanding, dependable, listening, stable, heavenly minded, priceless, persevering.* This is our Lord personified!

Fatal Footwear . . . Comfort Killers!

Callous People, Corny Folks, and a Fungus Among Us

By now you know I love *comfortable* shoes. I need comfortable shoes. That's what I look for in shoes . . . and in friends. But somewhere along the way, we have all had a pair of uncomfortable shoes hanging around our closet and our lives. Insensitive people are like uncomfortable shoes.

As much as a comfortable shoe beckons our feet to slip them on, the uncomfortable shoe sends our feet running in the other direction. Let's take a critical look at some uncomfortable shoes and see why they are not sensitive to our feet. Do they perhaps remind us of ourselves? If the shoe fits, it would be fitting to repent. No one would want to "wear us" if any of the following descriptions fit our behavior or attitudes.

The Infant Shoe

I'm not sentimental by nature, yet I display on a table my white leather baby shoes. When I see them, my mouth pulls into a nostalgic grin. I outgrew them when I was eighteen months old. When I was a three-year-old, my mother could've forced them on my little feet, but they would have been too confining for proper growth.

Often, we meet Christians who are what I'd call peripheral believers. Satisfied with hanging on to the outer limits of walking with God and wanting to remain on milk rather than graduate to meat, these precious babes in Christ may not be good for us. It is not that we are better than they, but that we need to mature rather than remain "cute." We have outgrown our baby shoes and developed beyond the consistent immaturity of a few people with whom we used to "toddle around." We are no longer comfortable confined to the playpen, but want to climb Mt. Everest! We long for our destiny not our Desitin. Rather than calling for Mommy, we want to cry out to the Father, asking for his help as we continue to mature on our respective Christian journeys. We do best when our central circle of friends, by example, encourages us to maturity. The carnal—the stunted friends—will not. They are content to nurse rather than feast.

Lord, show us if we ever have the "Infant Shoe" effect on others.

> *We have much to say about this, but it is hard to explain because you are slow to learn. In fact, though by this time you ought to be teachers, you need someone to teach you the elementary truths of God's word all over again. You need milk, not solid food! Anyone who lives on milk, being still an infant, is not acquainted with the teaching about righteousness. But solid food is for the mature, who by constant use have trained themselves to distinguish good from evil.*
>
> *Hebrews 5:11–14*

The "No Arch" Tennis Shoe

These tennis shoes look like Keds and slide on like Keds. I would've raised my right hand to swear, "To the best of my knowledge, these *must* be Keds." But, after one day in those shoes, I would've raised my right hand . . . to smack the shoe company. "These ain't no Keds!" How did I know? Real Keds have an arch.

These are *no arch* tennis shoes. When I want nothin' but flat, I'll wear socks. Hey, I'm not paying money for fakes that are missing the bump in the bottom. Flat and unsupportive! Who would've thunk it? These white tennies are a sorry copy of my great, well-worn Keds. (In fact, the pretenders are labeled "Kedz.")

During a tragedy we often realize we have a few "friends" who are not the genuine article. Though they know of our painful, often life-changing position, there is no card or call. Our first thoughts are, "The card got lost in the mail" or "They've moved to Greenland and are snowed in forever."

The *real* Keds in our circle of friends let us know they are aware of the pain. The giving goes beyond anything we ever imagined. Just receiving a

Hallmark card simply signed with their name is enough support and a sufficient, nurturing "bump in the bottom of the shoe."

All tennis shoes should have the essentials, like an arch. It doesn't have to be a big arch. Just something there to provide the basic, needed support. We often just need the simple communication of awareness that they know our pain. Otherwise, we might possibly conclude that what we thought was a Ked is really only a flat, insensitive soul.

Lord, show us if we ever have the "No Arch Tennis Shoe" effect on others.

But God, who comforts the downcast, comforted us by the coming of Titus, and not only by his coming but also by the comfort you had given him. He told us about your longing for me, your deep sorrow, your ardent concern for me, so that my joy was greater than ever.
2 Corinthians 7:6–7

The Showy Shoe

"Look at me!" shouts this fabulous footwear. Soooooooo fancy! A *knockout* of a shoe. This shoe steals the show with its overwhelming presence. This shoe wants to be "top dog" with all eyes on it!

Imagine a silver rhinestone pump with a purple velvet, fringed bow on the toes and transparent stiletto heels in which a goldfish swims. Who could help but notice such a shoe!!! The modest black leather pump hasn't a chance of competing on the dance floor with such over-the-top foot-fare.

Showy shoes are insensitive to the whole of what is going on. These shoes speak so loudly no one can hear anyone else. Perhaps the modest shoe wants a chance to make a statement like, "I want to make a statement!" But the flamboyant shoe has a hundred statements to make. Most may say the showy shoe has a glorious shimmer to it and brightens up the room. Yes, the extraordinary, shiny shoe with all the sparkles and fish were fun and entertaining doing the jitterbug. But . . . so overshadowing.

I shamefully confess I know what it's like to be a "sparkly shoe." In the past, I could match anyone with stories and statements. Mention anything from A to Z (Zenitz was my maiden name) and I would have a tale to tell. This particular shoe took its toe and pointed right at me.

Fear not. I've finally experienced enough mirror images of my extravagant gab to be gaining sensitivity towards others who may not care to hear of ten possible good uses for the hotel's free shower cap. Now, because of the work of God, I want to go only as far as the Lord directs, being aware when He is gently, quietly urging me to *SHUT UP*. (BUT—shower caps *may* be put to good use when wrapped around shoes to be packed in luggage.)

Lord, show us if we ever have the "Showy Shoe" effect on others.

When words are many, sin is not absent, but he who holds
his tongue is wise.
Proverbs 10:19

The Holey Shoe

At the end of a long, busy day, don't you just love throwing off your clothes and wrapping up in a cozy robe? And how about your tired feet? Isn't it the greatest feeling in the world to kick your shoes aside, and ease those squealing little piggies into a welcoming, soft bedroom slipper? Yet, there's something about being out of our clothes that makes us act *very careful even though carefree.* That's because we're exposed to some degree.

Bedroom slippers are like your closest friends. You can "bare your soul" totally to them. Knowing the naked you, both slippers and intimate friends provide a safe place to hang loose, to relax, and to be unguarded. They wrap themselves around us, inviting us to entrust ourselves to them for security and warmth.

Sadly, I've had to discard many pairs over the years. Since the fabric is often somewhat thin and delicate, it doesn't take too much for a small wear spot to develop. The damage always begins on the *inside* layer, where my toes have the closest contact with the slipper. Once a wear spot begins, with continued pressure it inevitably breaks through as a hole to the outside. The hole will allow the gathered warmth inside the slipper to escape and my foot will feel the chill.

My immediate response: to the dumpster with these drafty, disappointing slippers!

So it goes in our closest relationships. It feels so good to relax and let our most private self be known, safeguarded by the inner sanctum of friendship. But once a "wear spot" begins because of violated confidences, it's hard to repair. A rupture is sure to follow. What was meant to stay inside has escaped through the hole of broken trust. The warmth disappears. Our guard goes up, and we put our foot down, saying "I'll never share anything with her again!"

Lord, show us if we ever have a "Holey Shoe" effect on others.

If you argue your case with a neighbor,
do not betray another man's confidence . . .
Proverbs 25:9

A gossip betrays a confidence, but a trustworthy man keeps a secret.
Proverbs 11:13

The Man's Shoe

My shoe size is 8½. It's a narrow foot that requires a narrow shoe. If I try to walk in a wide shoe, it just doesn't work. My foot doesn't get the support it needs, and I wobble and stumble as a result. My narrow foot simply desires to walk in the "narrow" way.

One day I discovered an old pair of my husband's shoes in the dust-bunny-filled recesses of my closet. (I had given away all of Bernie's things after he died, so I was surprised to find them there.) Compared to my shoes, the contrast of their size and width caught my attention.

Just for fun, I slipped one on. It felt awkward and clumsy on my foot. It was so heavy and wide that my foot couldn't direct it. It was as if that shoe had a mind all its own. Despite my foot's intending to go one way, the man's shoe wanted to take me in quite another.

Some friends are like that. They'll entice you to walk in their shoes down broad streets paved with the world's promises. Take care to resist the temptation. Simply tell them you've got cold feet! The shoes that fit man's nature (I don't mean *men,* but all of *mankind*) will lead you down paths of self-effort, self-sufficiency, and vanity. Trying to find true, life satisfaction apart from God is a dead end street—literally!

Wearing man's shoe will inevitably cause your foot to slip. If you've got friends like that, make sure to keep them out of your circle of friends who are influencers.

Let this be our credo:
I don't want to walk in man's shoes. They don't fit me! And I don't want to go where they're heading. I'm a Christian. I know where God has directed me to walk. I have to be sure my shoes—and my friends—respect my need to stay on the straight and "narrow" way.

Lord, show us if we have the "Man's Shoe" effect on others.

Enter through the narrow gate. For wide is the gate and broad is the road
that leads to destruction, and many enter through it.
Matthew 7:13

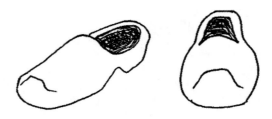

The Dutch Shoe

The Dutch shoe creates bunions, calluses, and corns. Don't you suppose modern-thinking Hollanders have set fire to most of these inhospitable clodhoppers? Their mantra for years was likely, "I can't wait to take these nutty clogs off! A few more windmills to pass, and I'll be home!"

I put a wooden shoe on this year. Talk about control! That inconsiderate shoe insisted on its own way. It was self-centered. No give. Not sensitive to what was going on with my foot. It was trying to shape my foot to its specifications. The playful expression, "If you ain't Dutch, you ain't much!" is this shoe's attitude. It unyieldingly demands rigid conformity. This rigid shoe clunks loudly on tile, but may just as easily be controlling, not making a sound, as it pads through a carpeted room.

I looked downward and spoke back to the wooden boats, "You will not imprison my dainty, soft, fragile feet—to the fireplace with you!" And, as it hit the flames it was still pontificating: **If I want your opinion, I'll give it to you!**

I've saved this "comfort killer" shoe for last. I've mulled over the thought that this shoe turns people off more than any other. Therefore, I shall be more lengthy (like a size 15D) about this toxic clodhopper.

Have you ever been in a conversation with someone who insisted, *as usual,* on proving that they were right about a point of fact or a debatable position? Whatever the topic, this self-assured, walking repository of all truth and wisdom argued her "rightness" until everyone either shut up (feeling overwhelmed and out-talked) or got up and walked away (feeling angry and controlled). It can be on any subject, but this person must *always* have the final *and* authoritative word.

When we must win the day with our "faultless" opinion, we in effect label all other points of view, and the people who present them, as flawed and inferior. This does not mean there can never be a "right" view. But the critical issue here is recognizing the value of those holding to a differing position. Being wrong at times (or at least graciously acknowledging that you *may be* wrong, even if you think you're not) makes you more human, approachable, and comfortable to be around.

Let's examine ourselves for such tendencies. Does being right *really* matter to us? We need to ask why, and pray about it. It's helpful to remind ourselves that God alone is right all the time. The rest of us are simply scratching the surface of truth. The Apostle Paul teaches us: "*Now we see but a poor reflection as in a mirror; then we shall see face to face. Now I know in part; then I shall know fully. . . .*" (1 Corinthians 13:12)

Allow space for you and others to be wrong, and for God to reveal the right answers to all in His time, and in His way. Relax. It's not a sin to admit you're wrong. And I know I'm absolutely *right* about that!

Lord, show us if we ever have the "Wooden Shoe" effect on others.

Then Jesus said to the crowds and to his disciples: "The teachers of the law and the Pharisees sit in Moses' seat. So you must obey them and do everything they tell you. But do not do what they do, for they do not practice what they preach. They tie up heavy loads and put them on men's shoulders, but they themselves are not willing to lift a finger to move them."
Matthew 23: 1–4

For I knew how stubborn you were; the sinews of your neck were iron, your forehead was bronze.
Isaiah 48:4

I end this section with this: A bad fit can make even the best shoes hurt. Walk a mile in these shoes? No Way!

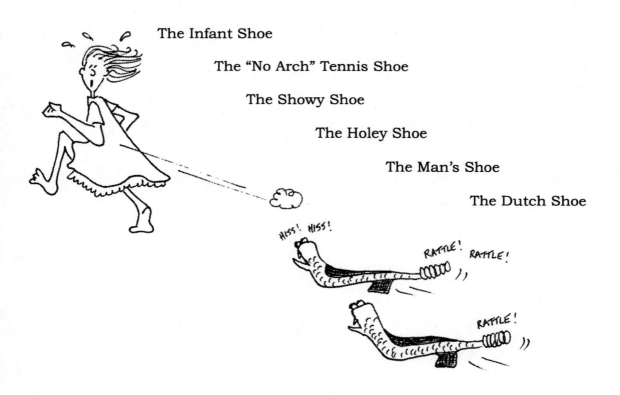

The Infant Shoe

The "No Arch" Tennis Shoe

The Showy Shoe

The Holey Shoe

The Man's Shoe

The Dutch Shoe

SECTION FIVE

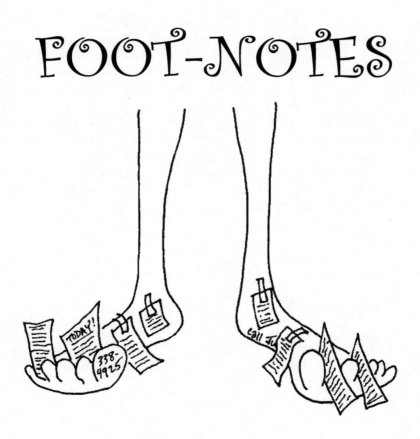

Fit for Comfort

So far, we have been able to try on the easy-walking, comfortable shoe; the not so welcoming, toe-pinching, foot-stomping shoe; and the supreme comfort and experience of the *Perfect Shoe* (Jesus Christ). Let's examine some of the ways to become more comfortable shoes. See if you can relate. And, as we grow from these experiences, we learn that God has graciously given us words of wisdom to guide us in becoming like unto—a comfortable shoe.

As you read these examples, realize my purpose is not the example, but the "footnote," which will provide you with tips on becoming a more comfortable person . . . for Christ's sake, of course.

Different Strokes for Different Folks

Do you wish everyone thought just the way you do, behaved just the way you do? Often our unspoken, subconscious expectation when we interact with others—whether family members, friends, or co-workers—is to have them respond to life just as we do. To like what we like, to see life through our lenses, to agree with our assessments and preferences. It's not a matter of control (Dutch shoe), but more frustration with others who are wired differently in temperament than we are.

I can't stop smiling when I think of the day I ordered all four of my teenaged children to clean their rooms. I gave them one hour. People were coming to traipse through our ranch home, to view each room. I had my own standard for a "shipshape" room—*my bedroom* was the prototype! My personality, my way of operating in life to get results, and my preferences became the final word on the how-to of cleaning a bedroom.

The hour passed and I made my way to Mark's room, the renowned "messy" in the Reamer clan. He saved every restaurant matchbook (didn't smoke), every lock of his hair from the barber, every paper, every magazine that he had ever held in his hands. I believe Mark would have saved every sunbeam that ever lit on his room if possible.

There was Mark sitting Indian style on the floor with a scrapbook opened in his lap. "Hi Mom, c'mon over here! Look at what I found. It is *so* cool!"

Every corner, every horizontal surface was still smothered with his paraphernalia. Nothing seemed changed. Clutter's Last Stand was still evident! "Mark! What are you doing?!? The hour is up and your room still looks like ten toddlers live in here!"

"Mom, I really am moving along and it'll be done, but when I started straightening, I came across my scrapbook which I haven't seen in ages! *Oh, come here, Mom,* and look at this page!"

Mark's way of cleaning meant he would be working on it the rest of his life, promising me that by the end of time, I would be really proud of his job well done.

Disappointed, I made my way to Jeff's room. The louvered doors opened wide to his closet. His clothes stacked and folded neatly and evenly. His hanging clothes coded by function and color. He showed me his bureau drawers. Same story. His organization of belongings was an A+. What an efficient plan he had to get his room uncluttered. But not cleaned! The dust was thick at every turn of my critical eye. The carpet was linty and untouched by a vacuum. But, he was organized . . . even if still dirty.

Disillusioned, I dragged my body to Jeff's twin, Jill's room. "Ah! A duster!" I found me a duster! Ah! A vacuumer! I found me the Vacuum Lady!" All the clutter was gone! I could see her floor, her bureau, her bed and her shining smile.

"I'm finished, Mom. It took hardly any time at all!"

Yes, she did pass the white glove test as dust was nowhere to be sneezed at, and the carpet had a "just installed" look to it. But then, but then, BUT THEN . . . as I tried to peek into her closet, I was suddenly attacked by hordes of wardrobe monsters jumping out at me, and only one drawer would open in the bureau. (The monsters had an iron grip on all of them too!) Under the bed were more monstrous piles of all the "stuff" a girl has in her room. Jill's idea of cleaning a room was to dust and vacuum and dispose of anything in the way of the rag and the Hoover by shoving it in the closet, drawers, or under the bed.

In despair, three children down and one to go, Johnny was my only hope for the day; I approached his door to see it closed. *"Why is his door closed when he knows I'm coming down the hall to view his presentation of a clean room?"*

The only presentation I got was a sign tacked to the door that read, "Don't disturb! Studying for finals."

I knocked and entered and saw the same room that I had seen an hour earlier, messy and dusty. "What is wrong with you, Johnny? I told you to get your room cleaned since people were coming over to see the house."

"I know, I know, Mom. But I figure if they see this sign they will turn around and walk away. Why clean the room if no one but me is going to be in here? There will be enough other rooms in the house for them to see."

I retired to my *perfect* bedroom, which was cleaned by *me,* in *my way,* according to *my measure* of what constitutes a clean room. I went over the four children and their four rooms in my mind. They had all responded to my request, convinced that I would be pleased with the way they went about the task. They knew I appreciated *joie de vivre* (vitality, enthusiasm), order, cleanliness, and creativity. And that's just what I got! Mark: *joie de vivre.* Jeff: order. Jill: cleanliness. Johnny: creativity. What was this saying?

In the world of psychology, there are many testing instruments that help to define personality type and temperament. Ultimately, they all point to the same conclusion: people are different from one another. We all have certain innate preferences that govern our modes of response to our world and dictate our behaviors.

Unfortunately, knowing this doesn't keep us from the temptation to self-worship. In the privacy of our mental confessional booths we admit, *I think the world would be better off if everyone were just a little more like me.*

The inclination to want to influence others to our own way of thinking, feeling, and doing never quits. But if we make someone who is *different* from us feel uncomfortable, we will undoubtedly see that "odd man" go away from us.

The Apostle Paul states, "I wish that all men were as I am." (1 Corinthians 7:7) In context, he is talking about his singleness and ability to devote himself completely to the work of the Gospel as opposed to being married. He would have preferred to see others live life with his same focus and intensity. But he quickly adds, "But each man has his own gift from God; one has this gift, another has that." God created us each uniquely and will work uniquely in each of our lives.

 Here's the Point:

Having a working knowledge of someone's basic personality traits, traditions, family background, and personal history is an advantage. Discovering those qualities may help us *understand any resistance* to the message we bear.

When we create an "odd man out" environment, it distances and divides. God's kingdom is all about drawing near in unity, not uniformity. How easily do we embrace the differences in others' personalities, giftings, and preferences? Do I actually think God will only deal with people who are just like me, in exactly the same way He has worked with me? *Really?* How odd!

Now the body is not made up of one part but of many. If the foot should say, "Because I am not a hand, I do not belong to the body," it would not for that reason cease to be part of the body. And if the ear should say, "Because I am not an eye, I do not belong to the body," it would not for that reason cease to be part of the body. If the whole body were an eye, where would the sense of hearing be? If the whole body were an ear, where would the sense of smell be? But in fact God has arranged the parts in the body, every one of them, just as he wanted them to be. If they were all one part, where would the body be? As it is, there are many parts, but one body.
1 Corinthians 12:14–20

Listen to Me, Please!

We've all become familiar with the investment firm that boasts: "When E.F. Hutton speaks, people listen." Lucky Mr. Hutton. Nothing can turn us off as fast as speaking to someone who hardly listens, who shows not the slightest degree of interest in what we have to say.

Everyone we meet has a story to tell. It's true! It's been said the sweetest sound in a person's ear is the sound of her own name. Perhaps next in order of sweet sounds would be to hear: "Tell me about yourself."

When around others, it's a sure bet we're not the only ones with something to say. With life experiences to relate. With opinions to air. With hurts to share. With discoveries to announce. A funny incident to tell. Let's remember how good it feels when someone *actively* listens to us. Then we'll be eager to extend that same wonderful gift. It's a *must have* skill if God is going to use us as effective messengers of His story.

Good listeners share some common qualities. They make us feel as if the earth's motor is temporarily unplugged. Nothing else matters for this slice of time. They don't slyly check their watch or consult their planner. No, they fully engage with us—eyes fastened on ours, ears open, mouth closed. We are the center of their universe, feeling validated, understood, worthy of their investment of interest and time.

Exhausted after speaking all day and at night at a conference, I retired to my hotel room. I had plans to reward myself by watching a PBS presentation on the ascent of Everest by a blind man. I had waited a month to view this. It promised to be as good as a box of chocolates, *dark* chocolates! The first ten minutes of the show were riveting. I was one happy camper, and I wasn't even in Nepal. As the climbers were ascending, so were my spiritual antennae. I was seeing the possibilities for a fresh teaching, applying this remarkable story.

Just then, the phone rang demanding a response. I knew who it would be: Bernie, my beloved spouse and faithful watchdog. "Hi Hon', how was the meeting? What have you eaten today? Have you talked to the children? Did you get my message earlier? Was the plane ride smooth? What's the weather like there? Have you met anyone at the retreat you knew before? Are they taking you to see nearby Mt. Rushmore? Did you have time to sew the button on your suit? Do you know you left your watch at home? Do you want me to respond to the three calls and six e-mails you've gotten? Do you know how much I love you? Do you want to know how your pregnancy test turned out? And guess what, I've got news about Jill's soccer scholarship and Johnny's CPA exam results! And let's see . . . what else can I tell you about my day and what's going on here? I'm ready to hit the sack. I just thought I'd give you a call before I close my eyes."

Knowing he was ready for bed, I couldn't ask him to call me back later. Yet every word of Bernie's was distracting me from the avalanches, crevasses, hypothermia, and altitude sickness that were beginning to overcome the blind climber. This was the program I had looked forward to watching for a month! Everest is one of my main fascinations, but Bernie was my main squeeze! And here I was, in a squeeze, myself! Bernie needed some unhurried time from a comfortable wife. Instead, he correctly sensed an *uncomfortable* wife with a *hurried* spirit. I had prioritized a mountain over my mate!

What do you do when a person needs your ear, and your own selfish desires want to climb another path? In this case, I let the heights of Everest cause me to descend into the valley of self-interest. I offended my precious husband. He could tell I was distracted and uninterested. He hung up quickly, and the program now meant nothing to me as I realized my sin. He needed, and deserved, my undivided attention.

Stephen Covey in his book *Seven Habits of Highly Effective People* says that often what happens when someone speaks is that others don't listen; they pretend to listen, listen selectively, or mentally begin readying their response. What appears to be listening may in reality be evaluating, probing, analyzing, and advising. Sound familiar? Hey! Wake up! Have you been listening to me?

 Here's the Point:

Good listening is perhaps the hardest work we can be asked to do by God. It requires silence. It requires concentration. It requires selflessness. It demands the active inspiration of the grace of God to shift my attention from me to someone else. But it is perhaps the most satisfying and fruitful labor of love. Because a good listener is a faithful messenger of God inaudibly announcing to the one being listened to: "I love you. I care about you. I'm interested in you."

Scripture is full of warnings about how we use our lips and our ears. Let's *listen!*

Everyone should be quick to listen, slow to speak . . .
James 1:19

Truth and Consequences

Recently my closest Jewish friend picked me up to attend a mini high school reunion held in Florida for those who had moved there or had second homes there. I happened to be in Florida at that time. (I would be the only follower of the Messiah among all these Jewish classmates.) As we drove, she warned about a potential problem awaiting me. Thirty years earlier, at another class reunion, the topic of divorce had come up. Apparently, although I had *no* recollection of it, I was being quoted as having said to another woman, "Anyone who has been divorced twice is going to Hell." Stung by whatever it was I said (and probably misunderstanding me), she did what some women do. She told another woman. And another.

Here I was looking forward to being among these old buddies when I learned that I was perceived as an *uncomfortable* person. My grand entrance with my stunning outfit and great hair day would be tainted with the vision of a black robed "judge" pointing my finger of TRUTH at all my divorced and remarried friends at the gathering. (And trust me, there were many in that condition!)

Who knows what I might have said three decades ago as a new Christian. Perhaps I was told of someone's pain because of a *second* divorce and said something as innocent (and true) as "Oh, that's why God hates divorce." But whatever it was, I now had to deal with the consequences of that mangled truth.

It seems there may be only two possible avenues of approach in such situations. One is to deny you ever said it and defend yourself at all cost! This is the "flesh" at work. The other is to go to the person(s) affected, apologize for the hurt caused, and take ownership of the words spoken, *even if* misheard or misunderstood.

Trying to find courage and steady my jangled nerves, I bathed my mind in this reassuring Scripture: "A gentle answer turns away wrath . . ." (Proverbs 15:1). Looking to exercise damage control, I simply said: "Sally, I am so sorry you have been hurt by something I said long ago. I truly don't remember the conversation we had. But if I said that then, I don't believe it anymore. Please forgive me."

I repeated that process a few times, gently taking aside other women who had also heard this damaging story. I didn't even try to give a corrected version of my "divorce statement." My goal was only to re-establish credibility as a *comfortable* person to be around. The rest would be up to God.

 Here's the Point:

Nothing is as powerful as the truth. But it can liberate or devastate, bring conviction or condemnation, heal or hurt. By its very nature, truth is bound to produce consequences. Jesus said, *" . . . you will know the truth, and the truth will set you free."* (John 8:32) We must be careful when we speak the truth, that it is God's truth, not our own corrupted version, and that we deliver it with sensitivity, grace, and the full consideration of its potential outcomes.

Be wise in the way you act toward outsiders;
make the most of every opportunity.

*Let your conversation be always full of grace, seasoned with salt, so that
you may know how to answer everyone.*
Colossians 4:5–6

Disputing Disputables

(Earlier, we talked about vexing people who always think they're right about everything from soup to nuts. In the following, we'll limit our discussion only to some of us *religious* nuts!)

In the movie *Lean on Me* (the true story of an inner-city high school resurrected from academic failure and social despair), the school's black principal "Crazy Joe Clark" is unfairly jailed. When the students learn of it, they protest in the streets, demanding his release. Fearing a riot, the city mayor urges Clark to go out and tell the students to go home. He presses Clark by saying, "You *have* to!" To which Clark responds, "I don't have to do anything *except* stay black and die!"

To be a Christian and claim the gift of eternal life, a person doesn't have to do anything *except* believe in the Lord Jesus Christ (Luke 23:32–43; John 6:28–29; Romans 10:9, Acts 16:30–31). Belief, of course, is not simply intellectual assent, but faith expressed in our surrender to His rightful Lordship. Happily for all of us, however, that doesn't mean we must possess a perfect understanding of the Bible or a flawlessly constructed theology to be a legitimate believer.

We may err terribly if we insist that, for someone to qualify as a *bona fide* believer, they must embrace particular points of view (which coincidentally just happen to line up with our own!) or certain rules of conduct.

Being a comfortable person means resisting the impulse to judge others by outward appearances or behaviors. That's hard to do because judging comes so naturally. Who of us would have selected Saul of Tarsus as the likeliest candidate to become God's super apostle? Look at his pre-conversion behavior, his ironclad Pharisaical attitudes!

Romans 14:1 finds this once highly questionable candidate for Christ's family now suitable to teach us, *"Accept him whose faith is weak, without passing judgment on disputable matters."* Implicit in this teaching by Paul is the truth that there are, in fact, disputable matters in the Christian life.

What might some of these disputable matters be? How about drinking alcohol, mode of baptism, end times theology (all those "mils"), smoking? And let's not forget the gifts of the Spirit and their operation today, the doctrine of election, eternal security. (Is it "once saved, always saved" or can a person lose their salvation?)

Here's an awful anecdote from my own walk:

I was baptized by Pat Boone in Las Vegas. Some disputed that my baptism was valid since a movie star placed me in the water, with the pastor standing off to the side. How hard that was for me, coming home from Vegas so intoxicated with the Lord, and then . . . Boom! Some began chiding me for letting Pat do the honors of my baptism. It sure hurt my little newborn heart, especially since I *knew* God had been the architect of the entire Las Vegas saga. I was certain of it! What does it matter *who* places me in the water as long as my comprehension of the purposes of the baptism is sound? Eventually I got over the attacks on my heart.

The issue of baptism was to raise its wet head once again when an evangelist came from England to stay with us. He disputed *not* Pat Boone's baptizing me, but *instead* the words Pat pronounced when he did it. Pat simply said, "In the name of the Father, Son and Holy Ghost, I baptize you." This British man sat on my sofa and told me all my present life problems were because I was not baptized *properly* with the words, "In the name of Jesus . . ." I highly esteemed this venerable man so I let him baptize me in my bathtub . . . *this time* in the name of Jesus only.

At that point, I began making phone calls insisting to the called ones that they needed to get over to my home before the man departed. "Let him baptize *you* in the *proper* way. You'll be delivered from all your long-standing strongholds! Come all ye faithful!" So the arguing and debating ensued. Disunity was occurring. Finally, two friends arrived and got into my bathtub. Singly, of course! We didn't have a Jacuzzi. In reality, we three women came out of the water and our same problems continued. The bathwater had not flushed us of the "flesh."

Can you imagine if I had allowed myself to be rebaptized *every time* someone with a different point of view about the *right* way to administer this sacrament came along? Good grief. I'd have webbed feet by now! (Of course, I'd be living up to the reputation I have among my Jewish friends: "Judy's all wet!")

Speaking of webs, what tangled ones we weave when we digress from the absolutes. Appalling arguments. Deathly disunity. Vicious vibes. Zealous to zonk others' particular views that differ from our own. Everything from A to Z.

Here's the point:

God is not resigning from His position as the Omniscient, Omnipresent, Omnipotent Ruler of the Universe. He's looked us all over from head to toe and found no candidates for succession to His throne. On His desk alone sits a sign that reads, "The Dispute Stops Here." Knowing how to disagree agreeably identifies you as a comfortable person.

> *May the God who gives endurance and encouragement give you a spirit of unity as you follow the Christ Jesus, so that with one heart and mouth you may glorify the God and Father of our Lord Jesus Christ. Accept one another just as Christ accepted you in order to bring praise to God.*
> *Romans 15:5–7*

"Here It Comes" Syndrome

When it comes to reputation, some Bible-believing Christians have earned themselves the description "a doozie!" And justly. They mean well, but they take the Gospel into the world like a gunfighter strolling into Dodge City at high noon.

Jesus has commanded us as believers to go into all the world and make (*not* shake 'n bake) disciples by sharing the Gospel. But he didn't suggest we should force it on *unwilling* hearers in an *uncomfortable* way. Yet in our zeal to be obedient to Christ, and out of a sincere desire for others to partake of the sweetness of the Lord, we sometimes push people further away.

It really *is* possible to be a silent ambassador of God's Living Presence. We don't have to verbally share the Gospel at every family reunion or Christmas dinner with our unsaved relatives. Nor do we need to put tracts in the hands of our new next door neighbors, or try to manipulate circumstances so we can give a "faith speech" to our son's soccer team.

In a much earlier season in my life, I truly believed I had the responsibility to share with everyone who crossed my path. I thought their salvation hinged on my boldness in some measure. So I always carried my testimony tape (in fact, a supply of them) with me and managed somehow or another to get it into the hands of whomever I'd meet.

But as I grew more sensitive to God's Spirit, He gently helped me to notice the discomfort I was creating in others. It was as if I could hear them saying to themselves, "Oh brother, here *it* comes," or more probably "Oh no, here *she* comes." No wonder. I was so focused on my own agenda, I paid no attention to either *their* readiness to hear the truth, or to whether the timing was *God's* timing. Scripture reminds us of the importance of seeing "conversion" as a process rather than a one-time event, and that God is sovereign over the outcome of our participation in that process. This is precisely what Paul means when he says, *"I planted the seed, Apollos watered it, but God made it grow. So neither he who plants nor he who waters is anything, but only God, who makes things grow."* (1 Corinthians 3:6–7)

 Here's the Point:

Relax, and, as they say, "Let go and let God!" He knows your heart and that you want to serve Him faithfully. So trust Him to handle the details on how and when someone will receive Christ. Have you been guilty of evangelism addiction? A sure sign of recovery from this attempt to try to control someone's salvation experience is when you can finally go to a family function and not have to teach, preach, or leave literature behind.

Love is patient, love is kind . . .
1 Corinthians 13:4

Overloading Circuits

When winter arrives, it is a given that at least a time or two, I will blow all the circuits in a room in my home. You name the room and I've done it there. Even the hallways suffer. I run too many electrical appliances at once along with my portable space heater. The wiring says, "I'm shutting down. Enough already with all these objects demanding my energy. No more juice for you, Judy!" The problem: overload.

If any of the comfort zone violations we've discussed in the preceding pages make me cringe, it's got to be this one. If I could put a sound to how awful I feel when I blow a *communication* circuit, it would come out "AAARRRGHH!" I've repeated this same *faux pas* over and over. When someone asks for an inch, I sometimes give a foot. And the foot I have left over is where? In my own mouth!

I have saved a letter I received years ago which causes me to groan "AAARRRGHH!" whenever I reread the words, but God has used it redemptively.

Here's the "letter encounter." The background is that the writer was a new "walker" (with Jesus) and she was living with her boyfriend. (Even now, I'm cringing as I type out some excerpts for you, but a little cringe is good now and then.) Read it (with my italicized emphasis) and you'll see why!

> *Dearest Judy,*
>
> *So many things I'd like to be able to express . . . I'll try! You have reached out to me and I know it is with the best intentions. God does put people in our lives on purpose. I have reached out to you in my new walk with God. There are many things I have to learn and understand and act*

upon. I have the desire for a close relationship with my Lord, and He is speaking to me in many wonderful ways.

Perhaps because I have opened myself up to you . . . you have responded too quickly to what you saw as a need to minister to me. You have given me tapes, books, and advice on counseling, weight loss, bible devotion, and to my significant other, a tape on his work.

I have the thinker, the doer, and the struggler mindsets and I think you felt I was in the achiever mode. You tested the waters on whether I was receptive . . . but I think a little too quickly to suggest "the fix."

Sometimes a person needs encouragement . . . to feel better about herself, to open their heart to God's Word . . . to consider the brighter side of the coin. And then it's up to them and God to move on to the next step.

After we got off the phone Thursday, I prayed hard, earnestly, and got a quiet voice . . . not a loud one and I relayed to Marvin the advice and admonition you offered. He was concerned for my sadness which was triggered by guilt. I don't believe God wants me to feel guilty. He wants the best for me . . . and wants me to reach for beauty out of desire, not out of fear. At least that's the God I know.

Please Judy, know that I treasure you . . . I just feel that I'm needing something different than your intense "how to's." Maybe my walk will be at a slower pace, and I will ask for forgiveness for my sins each day, but I shall continue to praise God for all I have now.

Let's take a little break from each other and I will pray for wisdom and guidance. You are loved . . . know that . . . I know you will pray for me!

Thank you, bless you,
Sheila (fictitious name)

A week later, her boyfriend told me off, very loudly, while at a buffet table in a hotel. I thought I would collapse in humiliation at the attack. (This was public. Mercifully, the letter was private.) I wanted to "soft shoe" out of there with the fastest tapping steps ever performed. Instead I sat at a table filled with witnesses to the tirade. I smiled at my food and inwardly cried out to God to give me wisdom on overloading people's circuits. That whole event was a marker forevermore.

 Here's the point:
Whenever a "Sheila" comes along who *asks you* a specific faith question, don't run away with it and answer with every bit of information you have, and every experience you've had, and every experience you know someone else has had! (Not to mention related religious rabbit trails, rebukes, recipes for righteous living and really helpful websites.) With your overload of "points," you've run with the ball to the opposite goalpost when they wanted you to stop at the ten-yard line on their end of the field. You thought you had scored a touchdown. Instead you incurred a flag on the play.

The basic rule to avoid overload? Follow the person *as far as you are certain they want to go* . . . and no further! If they won't go with you, what good is it? And most importantly, you may risk sacrificing the "comfort" factor.

"For my thoughts are not your thoughts, neither are your ways my ways,"
declares the Lord. "As the heavens are higher than the earth, so are my
ways higher than your ways and my thoughts than your thoughts."
Isaiah 55:8, 9

Tying Up Loose Ends

A word of caution and encouragement: *minister by the Spirit, not by techniques.* For example, suppose someone comes up to me in a meeting and says, "I'm Jewish, a friend brought me." I shouldn't whip out a Jewish slanted tract of the Four Spiritual Laws and start saying "Yeshua Hamaschiach, Ruach ha Kodesh," instead of using the name "Jesus." Not every Jewish person will respond to the Hebrew translation. It is unfair to treat someone as a commodity.

Before labeling them and finding a (shoe) box to fit them in, *wait and learn by questions, by friendliness.* Let's not go by traditions of men (robotic teachings we've learned). *Experience their uniqueness.* For instance, Jewish people "spew out" the idea of proselytizing. It is inconsiderate to go where they don't want to go at the start of a relationship. None of us want to be around someone who has an agenda for their life.

> *So in everything, do to others what you would have them do to you, for this*
> *sums up the Law and the Prophets.*
> *Matthew 7:12*

That's the secret to becoming a comfortable person.

Dwelling in us is the *most* sensitive person of all—the Holy Spirit. Pray for wisdom, and then . . . listen for Him! The way we deal with people may really affect their spiritual development, be it abundant growth or stunted growth.

If we discover we've been insensitive at any point, with humility (nothing to prove, fear, hide, or lose) we can say to the person in question, "I've been wrong. I'm so sorry I made you feel uncomfortable. I'm still growing up and learning, and it's a long process." Hooray for *faux pas!* This is how we all profit from our mistakes—learning by them that we may mature in Christ.

Footsteps to Follow

"If a relationship does not promote the kind of trust that inspires a person to invite us into his or her life, we have no real ministry opportunity."
—*Dr. James B. Richards*[4]

---

[4] Dr. James B. Richards, "How to Stop the Pain," Whitaker House

When I was young, I used to admire brilliant people. Now, I admire *comfortable* people. My late husband, Bernie, was very beloved and popular from his school days forward. He was a pleasure to spend time with. Our four children adored being around him because he was about as safe as you could ever hope for in a parent. And as a husband, he was as easy to be with as you might ever want in a spouse. (If he would only have eaten green vegetables, I could have sold him for millions on an auction block.)

There were sharper lawyers around. (My father was brilliant as an attorney and as a judge.) Yet, Bernie had the largest independent law firm in all of Baltimore. I clearly recognized he instinctively knew *the hidden value of being a comfortable soul.* That is what his clients felt about him: easy to talk with, a good listener, responsive.

Like Bernie, all of my shoe examples are comfortable people to be around for one reason or another. Yes, they all have outward graces, but I received two additional insights on something else they possessed. Firstly, regarding shoes, the comfort of a shoe is determined by the insole as well as possibly a soft leather covering and a good rubber crepe sole. Secondly, relating to man . . . a person may appear comfortable on the outside, but what is going on inside? Relaxed and resting are good words to describe the "in soul" activity of a comfortable person. Are we comfortable waiting . . . *waiting* for the divinely appointed moment to share what is burning in the heart? The good news of the Gospel of Jesus Christ.

Recently, I was shaken by a person's wrongful behavior. The Lord used this to show me that He provides the ultimate exemplary *"footsteps to follow."* I considered the Lord, since the hour was too late to reach out to a close friend. As I brooded over the troublesome, uncomfortable person, I questioned—

"Is there anyone in my life who doesn't have something wrong with him?!"
Sadly the answer came, NO! After a short pause came, I am included!

After I came to that conclusion, I experienced, as it were, a cloud parting
and a deeper revelation about how truly comfortable and safe our God is.
As I began to relax in His presence, I heard myself saying out loud,

"There is not one thing wrong with You, Lord.
There is not one thing wrong with YOU!"
I don't know of anyone else about whom I can say that.

I grabbed a piece of paper and proceeded to write down
the following thoughts:

No matter what the hour, You are always there when I need to talk.
I don't know of anyone else about whom I can say that.

You perfectly and fully identify with me when I am hurt and confused.
I don't know of anyone else about whom I can say that.

I never feel I am talking too much when, in vulnerability,
I open my heart to you.
I don't feel like that with anyone else.

You completely understand what I try to say
when words won't make it perfectly clear.
I don't know anyone else like that.

I can utterly trust You with secrets.
I needn't say, "I'll take your head off if this gets out!"
I don't know anyone else I can trust to the extent I trust You.

In the midst of strangers, I can walk in with my head held high.
I don't know anyone who can make that possible for me, except You.

If I were ever placed in solitary confinement,
I would not be living an isolated existence.
I don't know anyone but You who could be with me in captivity.

I am willing to make a "fool of myself"
by conversing with an invisible person . . . You.
I don't have any friend but You who could "faith" me enough to do that.

And with a grin I was able to write:
I can't allow anyone to get into the shower and sing with me . . . but You.

Is there anyone greater than Jesus Christ who can demonstrate the importance of being a comfortable and sensitive person? In order to put our best foot forward, may God's grace empower us to put on Christ . . . to be Christ-like to other people. Then, before that heavenly day when we come face to face with our Creator, we can hopefully present to Jesus others we have met along the way who, like us, now want to wear the Perfect Shoe.

The End

(Judy baring her soles)

Acknowledgments

I wrap my grateful arms around Donna Alberta, who wound her wisdom into these pages with me. A *comfortable* soul mate she is.

And . . . I draw no line in extolling the likes of Bobbie Wilkinson with her illustrative animations. If you want to *draw* her out she can be reached at bobbiewilkinson@earthlink.net. A *comfortable* artist she is.

And . . . I've pleasured in the heaps of skillful discernments of Donna Cornelius (Writeworks, Inc., writeworks@rcn.com) who took the piles of pages to the next step and made them print-worthy. A *comfortable* editor she is.

And . . . I hug heartily my newest friend, Sandy Feit, a reputable editor and writer who gave me her two cents and laughter whenever I would "ring her up" about the book. A *comfortable* "bubeleh" she is. (Pronounced "BOO-bahla": Jewish expression of endearment.)

All four pulled me upward and onward when I wanted to kick off my shoes and say "That's all, Folks!" As pooped to pop as I was at times, each of them got me back on my toes to turn a "spoken" message (my comfort zone), into getting the "big idea" into shape, hopefully to grace bookshelves far and wide.

There had to be a limit to the shoe metaphors used for this book, therefore I had to limit naming girlfriends who would aptly fit those similes. Not wanting to lose any of the *unmentioned* invaluable friends, here they are (alphabetically speaking): Barbara, Betty, Bev, Carole, Cathy, Diane, Jan, Jane, Joanna, Karen, Laine, Margie, Mary, Nancy, Ruth, Sadie, Sonja, Thelma, Shelley, and the entire *joined at the hip* Bible study gang.

And then there is my only daughter, Jill . . . words fail me. My daughters-in-law Eileen, Jackie, and Allison are close to my heart and are nothing less than that '50s word, *fabulous!*

If there's ever *The Parable of the Shoes, Part Two,* I would be able to easily connect those aforementioned names with some additional shoes (e.g., waist-high waders, wedding shoes, mountain boots, tap shoes) and some shoe accessories (e.g., clips, shoelaces, shoe polish). If you are one of my close friends and your name is missing, remember I have trouble locating my reading glasses, finding my car at a mall, and remembering to call or write you. I'm old. (Speaking of old, do you know what old is?? Old is when your friends compliment you on your new alligator shoes, and you're barefoot.)

In any case, my thanks to all of my precious friends, mentioned or not, for your lives being a living lesson to me on the hidden value of being a comfortable soul.